LAYERS OF LEARNING

YEAR ONE • UNIT FIVE

BABYLONIANS
MAPPING PEOPLE
HUMANS IN SPACE
POEMS ABOUT PEOPLE

HooDoo Publishing
United States of America
©2014 Layers of Learning
Copies of maps or activities may be made for a particular family or classroom.
ISBN 978-1494487850

If you wish to reproduce or print excerpts of this publication, please contact us at contact@layers-of-learning.com for permission. Thank you for respecting copyright laws.

UNITS AT A GLANCE: TOPICS FOR ALL FOUR YEARS OF THE LAYERS OF LEARNING PROGRAM

1	History	Geography	Science	The Arts
1	Mesopotamia	Maps & Globes	Planets	Cave Paintings
2	Egypt	Map Keys	Stars	Egyptian Art
3	Europe	Global Grids	Earth & Moon	Crafts
4	Ancient Greece	Wonders	Satellites	Greek Art
5	Babylon	Mapping People	Humans in Space	Poetry
6	The Levant	Physical Earth	Laws of Motion	List Poems
7	Phoenicians	Oceans	Motion	Moral Stories
8	Assyrians	Deserts	Fluids	Rhythm
9	Persians	Arctic	Waves	Melody
10	Ancient China	Forests	Machines	Chinese Art
11	Early Japan	Mountains	States of Matter	Line & Shape
12	Arabia	Rivers & Lakes	Atoms	Color & Value
13	Ancient India	Grasslands	Elements	Texture & Form
14	Ancient Africa	Africa	Bonding	African Tales
15	First North Americans	North America	Salts	Creative Kids
16	Ancient South America	South America	Plants	South American Art
17	Celts	Europe	Flowering Plants	Jewelry
18	Roman Republic	Asia	Trees	Roman Art
19	Christianity	Australia & Oceania	Simple Plants	Instruments
20	Roman Empire	You Explore	Fungi	Composing Music

2	History	Geography	Science	The Arts
1	Byzantines	Turkey	Climate & Seasons	Byzantine Art
2	Barbarians	Ireland	Forecasting	Illumination
3	Islam	Arabian Peninsula	Clouds & Precipitation	Creative Kids
4	Vikings	Norway	Special Effects	Viking Art
5	Anglo Saxons	Britain	Wild Weather	King Arthur Tales
6	Charlemagne	France	Cells and DNA	Carolingian Art
7	Normans	Nigeria	Skeletons	Canterbury Tales
8	Feudal System	Germany	Muscles, Skin, & Cardiopulmonary	Gothic Art
9	Crusades	Balkans	Digestive & Senses	Religious Art
10	Burgundy, Venice, Spain	Switzerland	Nerves	Oil Paints
11	Wars of the Roses	Russia	Health	Minstrels & Plays
12	Eastern Europe	Hungary	Metals	Printmaking
13	African Kingdoms	Mali	Carbon Chem	Textiles
14	Asian Kingdoms	Southeast Asia	Non-metals	Vivid Language
15	Mongols	Caucasus	Gases	Fun With Poetry
16	Medieval China & Japan	China	Electricity	Asian Arts
17	Pacific Peoples	Micronesia	Circuits	Arts of the Islands
18	American Peoples	Canada	Technology	Indian Legends
19	The Renaissance	Italy	Magnetism	Renaissance Art I
20	Explorers	Caribbean Sea	Motors	Renaissance Art II

3	History	Geography	Science	The Arts
1	Age of Exploration	Argentina and Chile	Classification & Insects	Fairy Tales
2	The Ottoman Empire	Egypt and Libya	Reptiles & Amphibians	Poetry
3	Mogul Empire	Pakistan & Afghanistan	Fish	Mogul Arts
4	Reformation	Angola & Zambia	Birds	Reformation Art
5	Renaissance England	Tanzania & Kenya	Mammals & Primates	Shakespeare
6	Thirty Years' War	Spain	Sound	Baroque Music
7	The Dutch	Netherlands	Light & Optics	Baroque Art I
8	France	Indonesia	Bending Light	Baroque Art II
9	The Enlightenment	Korean Pen.	Color	Art Journaling
10	Russia & Prussia	Central Asia	History of Science	Watercolors
11	Conquistadors	Baltic States	Igneous Rocks	Creative Kids
12	Settlers	Peru & Bolivia	Sedimentary Rocks	Native American Art
13	13 Colonies	Central America	Metamorphic Rocks	Settler Sayings
14	Slave Trade	Brazil	Gems & Minerals	Colonial Art
15	The South Pacific	Australasia	Fossils	Principles of Art
16	The British in India	India	Chemical Reactions	Classical Music
17	Boston Tea Party	Japan	Reversible Reactions	Folk Music
18	Founding Fathers	Iran	Compounds & Solutions	Rococo
19	Declaring Independence	Samoa and Tonga	Oxidation & Reduction	Creative Crafts I
20	The American Revolution	South Africa	Acids & Bases	Creative Crafts II

4	History	Geography	Science	The Arts
1	American Government	USA	Heat & Temperature	Patriotic Music
2	Expanding Nation	Pacific States	Motors & Engines	Tall Tales
3	Industrial Revolution	U.S. Landscapes	Energy	Romantic Art I
4	Revolutions	Mountain West States	Energy Sources	Romantic Art II
5	Africa	U.S. Political Maps	Energy Conversion	Impressionism I
6	The West	Southwest States	Earth Structure	Impressionism II
7	Civil War	National Parks	Plate Tectonics	Post-Impressionism
8	World War I	Plains States	Earthquakes	Expressionism
9	Totalitarianism	U.S. Economics	Volcanoes	Abstract Art
10	Great Depression	Heartland States	Mountain Building	Kinds of Art
11	World War II	Symbols and Landmarks	Chemistry of Air & Water	War Art
12	Modern East Asia	The South States	Food Chemistry	Modern Art
13	India's Independence	People of America	Industry	Pop Art
14	Israel	Appalachian States	Chemistry of Farming	Modern Music
15	Cold War	U.S. Territories	Chemistry of Medicine	Free Verse
16	Vietnam War	Atlantic States	Food Chains	Photography
17	Latin America	New England States	Animal Groups	Latin American Art
18	Civil Rights	Home State Study	Instincts	Theater & Film
19	Technology	Home State Study II	Habitats	Architecture
20	Terrorism	America in Review	Conservation	Creative Kids

www.layers-of-learning.com

Unit 1-5 Printable Pack

This unit includes printables at the end. To make life easier for you we also created digital printable packs for each unit. To retrieve your printable pack for Unit 1-5, please visit

www.layers-of-learning.com/digital-printable-packs/

Put the printable pack in your shopping cart and use this coupon code:

1213UNIT1-5

Your printable pack will be free.

LAYERS OF LEARNING INTRODUCTION

This is part of a series of units in the Layers of Learning homeschool curriculum, including the subjects of history, geography, science, and the arts. Children from 1st through 12th can participate in the same curriculum at the same time - family school style.

The units are intended to be used in order as the basis of a complete curriculum (once you add in a systematic math, reading, and writing program). You begin with Year 1 Unit 1 no matter what ages your children are. Spend about 2 weeks on each unit. You pick and choose the activities within the unit that appeal to you and read the books from the book list that are available to you or find others on the same topic from your library. We highly recommend that you use the timeline in every history section as the backbone. Then flesh out your learning with reading and activities that highlight the topics you think are the most important.

Alternatively, you can use the units as activity ideas to supplement another curriculum in any order you wish. You can still use them with all ages of children at the same time.

When you've finished with Year One, move on to Year Two, Year Three, and Year Four. Then begin again with Year One and work your way through the years again. Now your children will be older, reading more involved books, and writing more in depth. When you have completed the sequence for the second time, you start again on it for the third and final time. If your student began with Layers of Learning in 1st grade and stayed with it all the way through she would go through the four year rotation three times, firmly cementing the information in her mind in ever increasing depth. At each level you should expect increasing amounts of outside reading and writing. High schoolers in particular should be reading extensively, and if possible, participating in discussion groups.

☺ ☺ ☺ These icons will guide you in spotting activities and books that are appropriate for the age of child you are working with. But if you think an activity is too juvenile or too difficult for your kids, adjust accordingly. The icons are not there as rules, just guides.

☺ GRADES 1-4

☺ GRADES 5-8

☺ GRADES 9-12

Within each unit we share:
- EXPLORATIONS, activities relating to the topic;
- EXPERIMENTS, usually associated with science topics;
- EXPEDITIONS, field trips;
- EXPLANATIONS, teacher helps or educational philosophies.

In the sidebars we also include Additional Layers, Famous Folks, Fabulous Facts, On the Web, and other extra related topics that can take you off on tangents, exploring the world and your interests with a bit more freedom. The curriculum will always be there to pull you back on track when you're ready.

You can learn more about how to use this curriculum at www.layers-of-learning.com/layers-of-learning-program/

BABYLONIANS-MAPPING PEOPLE-HUMANS IN SPACE-POEMS ABOUT PEOPLE

UNIT FIVE

BABYLONIANS – MAPPING PEOPLE - HUMANS IN SPACE - POEMS ABOUT PEOPLE

We shall not cease from exploration and the end of all our exploring will be to arrive where we started . . . and know the place for the first time.
-T.S. Eliot

	LIBRARY LIST:
HISTORY	Search for: Babylonians, Ancient Babylon, Hanging Gardens, Hammurabi's Code, Nebuchadnezzar ☺ ☻ Ishtar and Tammuz: A Babylonian Myth of the Seasons by Christopher J. Moore. This is a children's picture book that is the Babylonian version of the Persephone myth. ☺ ☻ Gilgamesh the King, The Last Quest of Gilgamesh, and The Revenge of Ishtar by Ludmila Zeman. These three books are a trilogy about a king who goes on a quest for immortality. ☻ Ancient Mesopotamia: The Sumerians, Babylonians and Assyrians by Virginia Schomp. Filled with facts and pictures to engage. ☻ The Babylonians by Elaine Landau. Large type for kids to read with ease, covers the Babylonians in just the right amount of detail for the middle grades. ☻ The Story of Clocks and Calendars by Betsy Maestro. Western timekeeping begins with the ancient Mesopotamian people. This book ties together that distant past with today and stops at many other cultures and peoples along the way. ☻ Hammurabi: Babylonian Ruler by Christine Mayfield and Kristine M. Quinn. Biography of this very influential ruler. ● The Code of Hammurabi from Forgotten Books, publisher. This is the actual translated text of the code.
GEOGRAPHY	Search for: political maps, geography, maps, distribution maps, mapping ☺ Where we Live: Maps and Mapping by Susan Hoe. Basic explanation and activities on map making. ☺ ☻ The Everything Kids Geography Book by Jane Gardner and Elizabeth Mills. It really does have just about everything for the youngest kids. Use for the whole year. ☻ How the States Got Their Shapes by Mark Stein. The story of each state and how it got its borders. This is a fascinating look at the natural resources, political disputes, and poor surveying that's responsible for the crazy shapes of our states. ☺ Cartographia: Mapping Civilizations by Vincent Virga. Use this book as a reference and to browse through for its amazing maps and excellent explanations. ● The Map Book by Peter Barber. Beautiful full color maps and awesome explanations of human mapping through history. ● Mapping the World: an Illustrated History of Cartography by Ralph E Ehrenberg. Similar to The Map Book, this tells the history of human map making. ● To the Ends of the Earth: 100 Maps That Changed the World by Jeremy Harwood.

BABYLONIANS-MAPPING PEOPLE-HUMANS IN SPACE-POEMS ABOUT PEOPLE

SCIENCE

Search for: astronauts, telescopes, spaceships, space exploration, space probes

☺ Astronaut Handbook by Meghan McCarthy. Details on what it takes to be an astronaut.

☺ The Voyage of Mae Jemison by Susan Canizares and Samantha Berger. This picture book for young readers tells about the first African American woman to go into space. The main text of the book is extremely simple, but her whole story is detailed at the back.

☺ Astronauts in Space by Wil Spencer. This is a perfect independent read for a young reader. With only a few sentences per page, it tells the basics of everyday life for astronauts in space, including how they go to the bathroom!

☺ The Best Book of Spaceships by Ian Graham. Shows not only what various spaceships (mostly NASA) look like, but also how they work.

☺ ☺ The Hubble Space Telescope by Diane and Paul Sipiera. Tells the story of how the space telescope was put into orbit and what information it has given us.

☺ ☺ Voices From the Moon by Andrew Chaikin. A beautifully put together book filled with first hand accounts from astronauts who went to the moon describing their experiences. Includes beautiful photos.

☺ ☺ Space Shuttle: The First 20 Years from DK. Photographs and words of the space shuttle astronauts.

☺ ☺ Hubble: 15 Years of Discovery by Christensen and Fosbury. Stunning photos with explanatory captions. Hubble is arguably the most important space mission ever.

☺ We Seven by Carpenter, Glenn, Cooper, Grissom, Schirra, Shepherd, Slaton. This is the original 1962 account from the American astronauts who were part of the Mercury Program.

THE ARTS

Search for: Kids' poetry

☺ Read Aloud Rhymes For the Very Young by Jack Prelutsky, ed. Specifically chosen for pre-schoolers through about 2nd grade.

☺ ☺ Where The Sidewalk Ends by Shel Silverstein.

☺ ☺ A Light in the Attic by Shel Silverstein.

☺ ☺ Falling Up by Shel Silverstein.

☺ ☺ The Random House Book of Poetry For Children by Jack Prelutsky, ed. And Arnold Lobel, ill. Funny and fun book of children's poetry from dozens of authors.

☺ ☺ A Child's Garden of Verses by Robert Louis Stevenson. Beautiful poems that relate directly to the world of a child, but without being condescending or too light. Stevenson is a master of language. Memorize one or two of these.

☺ ☺ ☺ Kids Magnetic Poetry Book and Creativity Kit by Dave Kapell and Sally Steenland. A whole course on how to use words for great effect in poetry. Includes magnetic word tiles to create poems on the fridge or the magnetic pages of the book. Beware, buy new if you buy or the tiles will probably be missing, making the book useless.

☺ ☺ Walker Book of Classic Poetry and Poets by Michael Rosen, ed. A grown-up poetry book for your teen, this anthology contains poems written in the English language from Shakespeare to Judith Wright, in chronological order plus beautiful illustrations.

BABYLONIANS-MAPPING PEOPLE-HUMANS IN SPACE-POEMS ABOUT PEOPLE

HISTORY: BABYLONIANS

Additional Layer
The Babylonians worshiped many different gods. This is called pantheism. "Pan" means many in Latin. Learn about the different major categories of religion: pantheism, monotheism, animism, and polytheism.

Famous Folks
Astarte was one of the goddesses of the Babylonian religion. She was the goddess of fertility and war. Later she was called Aphrodite by the Greeks.

Fabulous Fact
There are two distinct Babylonian periods: 1867 BC to 1750 BC was the Old Babylonian Empire.
From 612 to 539 BC was the Neo-Babylonian Period.

The Babylonians under Hammurabi conquered the Sumerians and took over control of the Mesopotamian area. Their capital was at Babylon on the Euphrates River. Hammurabi wasn't the first king to make laws, but his are the most famous of the early laws. Often rulers have made arbitrary decisions, making things up as they go along. In Babylon it was different. If you broke a law, you knew exactly what the punishment would be, and of course you knew what was against the law in the first place.

Not long after Hammurabi died the Babylonians were taken over by other tribes, but the empire lived on and reached greatness under Nebuchadnezzar. Greatness in an empire means fighting lots of wars and conquering lots of people, and that's what the Babylonian emperors tried to do. One of the tribes they conquered was the Israelite tribe, a people whose story is told in the Bible. The Babylonian Empire lasted about twelve hundred fifty-three years from 1792 BC to 539 BC when it was conquered by the Persians.

🙂 🙂 🙂 **EXPLORATION: Map**
Use the Babylonian Empire map from the end of this unit. Color the various nations in the Middle East and then mark the area of the greatest extent of Babylonian dominion.

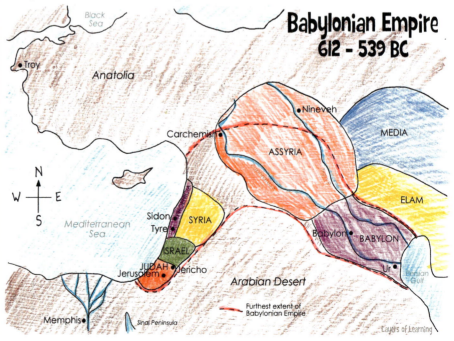

BABYLONIANS-MAPPING PEOPLE-HUMANS IN SPACE-POEMS ABOUT PEOPLE

☺ ☺ ☺ EXPLORATION: Timeline

You will find printable timeline squares at the end of this unit to post on a wall timeline or in a notebook timeline. All of these dates are B.C.

- 1764 Hammurabi conquers Elam
- 1763 Hammurabi makes Babylon his capital
- 1600 Hittites sack Babylon
- 1125-1104 Nebuchadnezzar I reigns
- 689 Assyrians destroy Babylon
- 652-648 Babylonians rebel against Assyrians
- 612 Medes and Babylonians ally to destroy Assyria
- 587 Nebuchadnezzar II captures Jerusalem and Judah becomes a province
- 586 Exile of Jews to Babylon
- 586 Babylonia conquers Phoenicia
- 581 Babylon burns Jerusalem
- 557 Ishtar Gate Built
- 550 Hanging Gardens built
- 539 Cyrus the Great conquers Babylon and frees Jews

☺ ☺ EXPLORATION: Chronology of Mesopotamia

In Unit 1-1 we learned about the "land between two rivers" and the first civilization we know of that lived there, the Sumerians. Now we speak of the Babylonian Empire, which is located in the same area. There are also the Elamites, the Akkadians, the Assyrians, the Hittites, the Semitic nomadic tribes, the Medes and the Persians and others who all ruled over this land or were near neighbors at some point. Besides all of that, there are alternate names for all these people depending on who you talk to. The Babylonians were also called the Chaldeans (beginning with a hard "K" sound).

Complicating it even further, we tend to insert our experience with modern nations into the ancient concept of empires, but they didn't function in the same way. Everyone (except visitors) who lives within the borders of France is considered French and has the rights and privileges as well as the responsibilities of all Frenchmen regardless of heritage, language, religion, or other factors. But ancient Babylon included Assyrians, Semites, Jews, and many other smaller tribes that never considered themselves Babylonian. The empire always functioned as a conquering nation over the people they administered. While the Babylonian Empire existed, the conquered nation of Israel existed simultaneously and in the same space. Even if you were actually a Babylonian and a citizen, you would have probably felt more affinity for your city or town than the Empire, so people were called things

Explanation

The whole point of studying history to is to study humans – who we are, how we behave, and how we treat each other. We look for patterns that give us clues as to what makes people tick. If we can understand at least a little, we can guard against the greater atrocities that have cropped up all too frequently in the history of the world.

We are fortunate to live in a time when we have more knowledge of past ages and greater access to that knowledge than ever before among any people on Earth. If we choose to take advantage of our access to knowledge then we need not suffer under oppressive governments or be subject to tyrants. But most people now days seem to hate history, so tragically we may be doomed to repeat our mistakes after all.

History repeats itself not because of some mystic cyclical fate of the universe, but because humans are the same people we were thousands of years ago. We are Babylon.

Michelle

Babylonians-Mapping People-Humans in Space-Poems About People

Additional Layer

There are four major groups of peoples that affect the early Mesopotamian region:

- Semites
- Indo-Europeans
- Egyptians
- Sumerians

These are language groups probably descended from their common ancestor or family.

The Semites claim descent from Shem, a son of Noah. The Egyptians claim descent from Ham, Noah's son. The Sumerians claim descent from Nimrod (of the Bible). The Indo-Europeans are more problematic since their culture, though we can find traces of it, has not been preserved in writing or myth.

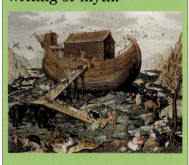

Fabulous Fact

The Greeks called it "Babylonia" but the locals called it "*Mât Akkadî.*"

like Abram of Ur, rather than Abram the Sumerian. It can be really difficult to fit the different people all into this space in your mind and sort out who goes where and when. Now is a good time to get that straightened out.

1. The **Sumerians**, a unique indigenous people begin the 1st civilization, establish divine kingship, city-states, a law code, a polytheistic religion, and high degree of commerce and wealth, making the neighbors envious.
2. The **Akkadians**, a Semitic people from Arabia, move in and conquer Sumer, but adopt all the Sumerian culture and government customs. The old Sumerian people still live there and are involved in government and religion and all the same stuff they used to do, but have to pay taxes to the Akkadians and do business in their language, most irksome. The Akkadians rule from Akkad.
3. **Sumer** regains control for about a century.
4. The **Amorites**, another Semitic tribe, take over the region, re-name Akkad "Babylon" and also become Sumerized. They are considered the first Babylonians. The Sumerian and Akkadian people still live in the area and, of course, hate all the usurpers, causing grief and unrest from time to time.
5. The **Hittites**, an Indo-European people, ride in on their chariots from the north, take over everybody from the Persian Gulf to the Levant, adopt everybody's gods (just to be on the safe side) and remain aloof from the people they have conquered.
6. The **Kassites**, another Indo-European people ride in on horses from the north, push the Hittites back to Anatolia, refuse to adopt the Sumerian culture, and are very short-lived as an empire.
7. The Semitic **Assyrians**, who had established city-states north of the Sumerian homeland, finally got their moment and conquered the region. They adopted much of Sumerian culture, but were more ruthless in their conquering than others had been. They also thought that forced migrations would help keep all that revolting under control.
8. **Babylon** reemerges as the dominant force and with the help of another Semitic tribe from the northeast, the Medes, they conquer the Assyrians. Babylon rules for a while, but continually has problems with revolting cities, which weakens it. Babylon itself welcomes the Persians into their gates. Of course, all the previous peoples and others who never did hit the big time are living within the borders of the Babylonian Empire and keeping their identities alive.
9. **Persians** march in from the east, with very little resistance in most places, and establish order and civilization again

Babylonians-Mapping People-Humans in Space-Poems About People

where all had turned to revolt and chaos under the Babylonians. But the Persians get greedy and head on into Greece . . . which turns out to be a bad move.

10. **Alexander the Great** unifies the Greek peninsula and then proceeds to conquer the rest of the known world from Egypt to the borders of India. The Greeks establish settlements, maintaining their own culture and identity, but influence the locals only a little. The ones most influenced by the Greeks were not to be those they conquered, but their conquerors, the Romans.

Write each of the bold names above on index cards and place them on a map of the Mediterranean region (a simple hand drawing on a board works fine) as you talk about each in turn.

😊 😊 😊 **EXPLORATION: Hammurabi's Law**

Hammurabi's Law is famous as a very early example of a written code of laws. Write up your own code of laws and punishments for your house or for your town or state. Include not only what the rules are, but also what the punishments to violators will be.

Some of Hammurabi's laws included:

- Anyone who commits a robbery will be put to death.
- Anyone who puts out an eye of an equal will have his eye put out.
- Anyone who knocks out the teeth of an equal will have his teeth knocked out.
- If a son strikes his father his hands will be cut off.
- If a man strikes a pregnant woman and causes her baby to die then the assailant's daughter will be put to death.

What do you think of these laws? What are the based on? What were the laws you wrote based on? Did you feel powerful as you wrote them?

😊 😊 😊 **EXPLORATION: A Fertile Land**

The Greek historian Herodotus described the land between the two rivers like this:

So great is the fertility of the grain fields that they normally produce crops of two-hundredfold, and in an exceptional year as

---

Fabulous Fact

Most people, both women and men, in ancient Babylon had at least some schooling and could read and write. There were libraries in every town. The more learned also studied the "dead" language of Sumerian as well as their own. They also had to study mathematics. But if you were an Assyrian from the north you were probably off the hook, unless you were very wealthy.

Additional Layer

Because of the Bible the term "Babylon" when used today often indicates a dissipated, corrupt society, the epitome of evil, which must be guarded against or embraced depending on your persuasion.

Look for modern day references to Babylon. What has the ancient city of Babylon been compared to and why?

Additional Layer

In lands with a "Rule of Law" there are written laws which are predictable, known, and consistent. In lands without written laws, justice can be subject to the whim of the ruler. Which sort of land do you want to live in?

Babylonians-Mapping People-Humans in Space-Poems About People

Fabulous Facts

The old Babylonian Empire covered the extent you see here:

The Neo-Babylonian Empire was much larger and covered the extent you see here:

Additional Layer

The Babylonian economy was based on agriculture primarily. They grew plenty of food to trade with the neighbors. What is your country's current economy based on? What do you sell to foreign countries?

much as three-hundredfold. The blades of wheat and barley are at least three inches wide. As for millet and sesame, I will not say to what an astonishing size they grow, though I know well enough; but I also know that people who have not been to Babylonia have refused to believe even what I have already said about its fertility.

Herodotus had never been there of course, but he interviewed many people. Do you believe his description or do you think he may have exaggerated?

Write an exaggerated account of the natural beauty, fertility or economic activity of your area.

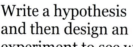 **EXPERIMENT: The Seeder Plow**

One of the reasons the Fertile Crescent was so fertile was the seeder plow. The Babylonians believed that the god Enlil invented the seeder plow and they could see its constellation in the night sky. It was a wooden plow that had a hollow funnel running down the middle of it. As the plow pushed through the soil it dropped seeds through the funnel and directly into the soil. During this period, and long after, the Mediterranean world used broadcast sowing, which means they plowed the ground and then threw the seeds out over the surface of the soil. Compare the different methods of planting. Which do you think would have greater yields? Which do you think would waste more seeds?

Write a hypothesis and then design an experiment to see which method will result in more seed germinating into plants.

EXPLORATION: Hanging Gardens

It is thought that the famous Hanging Gardens of Babylon was a Ziggurat with stepped levels. It was one of the original seven wonders of the ancient world. It was built by Nebuchadnezzar II for his Persian wife who was homesick for the trees and flowers of Persia. Sadly, the gardens were destroyed by earthquakes.

Build a model of the Hanging Gardens from saved boxes. Stack

Babylonians-Mapping People-Humans in Space-Poems About People

An engraving of the Hanging Gardens of Babylon by Dutch artist, Martin Heemskerck

the boxes one on top of the other and tape them together. Paint the whole thing out in a light brown. Then add artificial or real pieces of plants to show the gardens. You can paint streams and pools and waterfalls on the different levels as well.

There's paper model kit you can download and print out for free at http://www.delta7studios.com/garden.htm.

☻ ☻ **EXPLORATION: Ishtar Gate**
Nebuchadnezzar II also caused a great gate to be built upon the processional way through the wall of the inner city. He dedicated the gate to the goddess Ishtar. It was covered with blue glazed tiles and images of aurochs and dragons.

Famous Folks

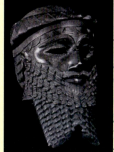
Sargon's step-dad was a gardener, but Sargon gained notice of the king and became his cup-bearer. Here is Sargon's autobiography:

My mother was a high priestess, my father I knew not. The brothers of my father loved the hills. My city is Azupiranu, which is situated on the banks of the Euphrates. My high priestess mother conceived me, in secret she bore me. She set me in a basket of rushes, with bitumen she sealed my lid. She cast me into the river which rose over me. The river bore me up and carried me to Akki, the drawer of water. Akki, the drawer of water, took me as his son and reared me. Akki, the drawer of water, appointed me as his gardener. While I was a gardener, Ishtar granted me her love, and for four . . . years I exercised kingship.

Sargon was the first of the Mesopotamians to unite many lands into one great empire.

Babylonians-Mapping People-Humans in Space-Poems About People

This is a Babylonian tablet containing a creation story and story of a great flood among other things.

Fabulous Fact
The Babylonians were trilingual. They used their own Semitic language for everyday, the Akkadian language for government, and the otherwise defunct Sumerian language for their religious ceremonies, like the Europeans later used Latin in the church.

Additional Layer
The study of the stars began with the study of astrology. The king wanted to know when a bad omen would appear, like an eclipse or a planetary transit. So wise men and priests would study the sky and make charts and learn to predict and read the heavens. Contrast astrology with astronomy.

Every New Year's celebration parade passed through this gate with images of the gods carried along on the shoulders of slaves. An auroch is a sort of bull and the Babylonian dragons were wingless.

An Auroch

Build a simple Ishtar gate out of a small cardboard box, like from gelatin dessert. Cut an arch out of the center and paint it out in blue. Paint tiny yellow dragons and bulls on the front. You can make the second layer of the gate from a slightly larger box.

You'll find an Ishtar Gate coloring page in the printables sections at the end of this unit. You can also purchase a paper model of the Ishtar Gate from paperlandmarks.com.

☺ ● EXPLORATION: Marduk and the Monster
Marduk was one of the most important of the Babylonian's gods. Nearly every culture around the world has a creation myth that has parallels to the creation story we read in the Bible. The Babylonians believed that Marduk sailed on a raft around the ocean, sprinkling dust on it to create the landforms. They also believed he created the first calendar and humans. They also believed he saved the whole world from a terrible sea monster named Tiamat.

Make your own sea monster using 1 large and 4 small paper plates, construction paper, scissors, glue, a hole punch, and pipe cleaners. Start by painting the plates green. Now add stripes to the plates using strips of construction paper of various bright colors. You may want to cut them in curves, fringes, or zigzag edges to make the stripes more interesting. Punch holes in the sides of the paper plates and attach them together using short pieces of

BABYLONIANS-MAPPING PEOPLE-HUMANS IN SPACE-POEMS ABOUT PEOPLE

pipe cleaner. Add eyes and a mouth to one small plate to be the sea monster's head, and then cut flames to come out of its mouth.

☺ ☻ **EXPLORATION: Akitu, The Babylonian New Year**
For the Babylonians, the new year (called Akitu) began in the spring, about late March or early April according to our calendar. They had a 12 day long festival, which was very religious in flavor. The high priests opened the festival, the statues of the gods were paraded through town in a procession, certain rituals were done with the king, and the people partied, ready for another great year blessed by the gods. The party lasted way beyond the Babylonians and into the Roman Era. For the Babylonians it marked not only spring, but also Marduk's victory over Tiamat the dragon.

Research more about Akitu and make a book with 12 pages, one for each day of the festival.

☺ ☻ **EXPLORATION: Babylonian Calendar**
The Babylonian calendar began in the spring, at the end of March or the beginning of April according to our calendar. The year was divided into three seasons of four months each, giving a total of 12 months. Each month was based on the lunar cycle beginning when the new crescent moon was sighted low on the horizon, giving 28 days per month. That left the year just a little short, since 12 lunar cycles is just under a solar year, so by decree they would insert intercalary days in when needed. Intercalary just means "inserted into the calendar." They were the extra days that needed to be added before the year cycle would be back on track. The calendar never seems to come out perfectly even, no matter how we make it. That's why we have leap years today.
The chart below shows the 12 months with their names and the intercalary period inserted when needed. Make your own Babylonian calendar chart with the printable from the end of this unit.

Famous Folks

The Babylonians invented a new god to take the place of the former supreme god, Enlil. The new supreme god was called Marduk, but most often was referred to as Bel or Baal, which means Lord. The Jews spoke of Bel most disparagingly in the Old Testament.

Writer's Workshop

Write your own creation story after you've read the story of Marduk and Tiamat.

Famous Folks

Amytis was the wife of King Nebuchadnezzar. She married him to cement the diplomatic relationship between Babylon and the Medes. He built the Hanging Gardens for her.

Babylonians-Mapping People-Humans in Space-Poems About People

Fabulous Fact
Sometimes the Babylonians as a whole are called the Chaldeans, but the term really refers to the priests who watched the heavens for bad omens.

On The Web
Michael Streck of Cambridge University speaks ancient Akkadian (with a British accent of course). Go listen to the incantation for a dog bite here:
http://upload.sms.csx.cam.ac.uk/media/759237

Famous Folks

Nabonidus was the last king of the Neo-Babylonian Empire. He seized power from the guy before him and ignored the god Marduk while faithfully worshiping the moon god, of whom his mother was a priestess, thereby committing political suicide.

Photo by Jona Iendering

Paste the months, seasons, and intercalary days on to your calendar.

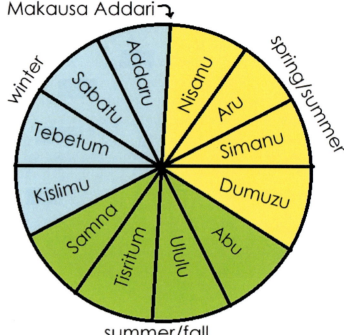

Babylonian Calendar

☺ ☻ **EXPLORATION: Mathematics**
The Babylonians used a base 60 system for mathematics, which we still use when we tell time or discuss the degrees of a circle. They also multiplied differently than we do today, probably because of their base 60 system. We multiply a x b and memorize the times tables. For example 5 x 4 = 20. If you were a Babylonian though you would use this formula to multiply:

$ab = [(a + b)^2 - (a - b)^2]/4$ (they had massively huge tables with the squared numbers listed up to 59 squared)

So if we're multiplying 5 times 4 we would think:
$[(5+4)^2 - (5-4)^2]/4$
$[(9)^2 - (1)^2]/4$
$[81 - 1]/4$
$80/4 = 20$

See, we got there eventually. Try some others in the Babylonian style:
    6 x 7   3 x 9   2 x 6   17 x 31

It's in the big numbers that our base ten system is really useful with its place holding capability. Use your calculator to find the squares of these big numbers.

BABYLONIANS-MAPPING PEOPLE-HUMANS IN SPACE-POEMS ABOUT PEOPLE

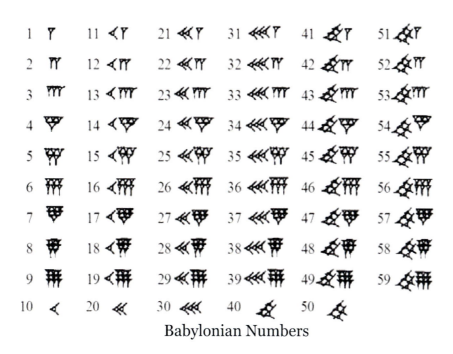

Babylonian Numbers

Famous Folks

Engaldi was the daughter of King Nabonidus. She ran a priestess school for women, opened the first museum of antiquities in the world, and spent a great deal of time as priestess to the moon god.

These are the foundation stones of Engaldi's Museum.

Photograph by M. Lubinski

🙂 😃 **Exploration: Ancient Civilizations Lapbook**

There's a great ancient civilizations lapbook example at ttp://www.tinasdynamichomeschoolplus.com/2013/06/05/ancient-civilizations-unit-minibook-on-the-babylonians-hammurabi/. This would be a terrific culmination activity for this unit that could combine a lot of the things you've learned into one project. You can even include what you've learned over the past several history units to see all that was happening in one context.

😃 **EXPLORATION: Ancient vs. Modern Research Project**

Today the land of Mesopotamia is one of the most discussed areas of the world. Anciently, it was also a warring area filled with a lot of political ambition. The Middle East region frequents our modern news reports, and if there were "news reports" back in ancient times, the Middle East would have been hot topic then too. Write a research paper comparing Middle Eastern past to Middle Eastern present. What do you think makes some areas more vulnerable to conflict while others are able to keep more peace and stability?

Fabulous Fact

This is Babylonian art carved into stone depicting Marduk with a king of Babylon. The king is showing obeisance to Marduk.

BABYLONIANS-MAPPING PEOPLE-HUMANS IN SPACE-POEMS ABOUT PEOPLE

GEOGRAPHY: MAPPING PEOPLE

On The Web

For a fascinatingly unique look at some curiositites of human mapping visit

http://bigthink.com/blogs/strange-maps

This is one blog worth subscribing to if you find maps the least bit interesting.

There is also a book by the blog's author, Frank Jacobs, called *Strange Maps*.

Fabulous Fact

A cartogram is a purposely distorted map of a physical place that is used to show a specific set of data.

This is a cartogram of the European Union showing the relative populations of member countries.

Additional Layer

Look in your student atlas at a map of your country. What distribution maps are included?

Besides just mapping the physical features of the earth, we like to map people too. When mapping people we can show man made things like roads, cities, buildings, man made boundaries, and so on. Maps showing these things are called political maps.

A political map shows the boundaries of countries and other artificial lines and marks on Earth. These are man made boundaries and can include countries, capitals, and other important cities, as well as anything that humans have built on the earth. Country borders change and people build or abandon cities and roads and dams, meaning that political maps can quickly grow out of date. Political maps can be simple or complex depending on how much detail they show.

Map makers also like to show where different religions flourish, or the places we can find the oil or timber we want, or how well educated different countries are. These are called distribution maps.

This map shows the distribution of countries which adopted the Cyrillic alphabet.

17

BABYLONIANS-MAPPING PEOPLE-HUMANS IN SPACE-POEMS ABOUT PEOPLE

Distribution maps are excellent if you want to show trends or resources that people like to use. Having a map can give you the big picture and help you spot patterns that you could not otherwise see.

☺ ☺ **EXPLORATION: Political versus Physical**
Most student atlases will show both political and physical maps of places in the world. Look at a map of South America in both the political and physical view. What does the political map show that the physical map does not? What is a political map useful for? Examine the two types of maps and have a discussion.

☺ ☺ ☺ **EXPLORATION: Political Mapmaker**
Create a map of a real or imagined place that includes man made items. Make a key showing the features you are including. Here are some things you may consider including:
- railroad tracks
- important buildings
- roads
- campgrounds
- airports
- museums
- college campuses
- parks

☺ ☺ **EXPLORATION: Four Colors**
Cartographers can use as few as four different colors to show countries or states without any colors sharing the borders. Pick four colors and color in a modern political map of Africa using only those four colors. Try to not let the same colors be neighbors. How difficult is it?

A map of Africa is in the printables at the end of this unit.

On the Web
Visit http://www.maps.com/funfacts.aspx to play a variety of online map games to help your kids get familiar with the world in a painless way.

Famous Folks
Henry Charles Beck was an employee of the London Underground when he designed a new map for the users of the underground. Old maps had been based on actual geography like this:

Beck redesigned and simplified the map, which is still in use, by ignoring actual geography and making the map into a schematic, similar to this one:

BABYLONIANS-MAPPING PEOPLE-HUMANS IN SPACE-POEMS ABOUT PEOPLE

Additional Layer

Political maps can sometimes be very, well, political. The darling of the publishing world is the Mercator projection, but the Mercator projection, though necessary for naval navigation, drastically distorts the size of continents as they get nearer the poles. On a Mercator Projection Greenland looks to be about the same size as Africa, but the truth is very different. Some people say this distortion of maps has caused prejudices and fueled dismissal of the large countries and populations near the equator, almost all of which are less-developed than their northern neighbors. A solution in the form of the Gall-Peters Projection has been proposed by cartographical activists.

What do you think? Is the form our maps take vital to justice and understanding on our planet or do these people have way too much time on their hands?

☺ ☺ ☺ EXPEDITION: Finding My Own Way

Go visit a place in your city that has a map to follow. This could be an amusement park, a zoo, or even a shopping mall. Mark several destinations on the map, then have the kids use the map to lead you to the destinations all on their own. If you had a physical map of the same area, would it help you find your way in this man made place?

☺ ☺ ☺ EXPLORATION: Political Asia

Answer these questions using a political map of Central Asia from an atlas:
1. Which central Asian country has Ashgabat as its capital city?
2. Which country is north of Tajikistan?
3. Name all the countries that border Afghanistan.
4. Find the capital city that is located at 42°N latitude, 75°E longitude.
5. What are the coordinates for the capital city Kabul?
6. Which country do you think took its name from a Mongol named Oz Beg Khan?

Now choose another political map from the atlas and create your own questions like these for someone else to find answers to.

☺ ☺ EXPLORATION: How The States Got Their Shapes

Within the United States, some of our most important political boundaries are our states' borders. Read *How the States Got Their Shapes* by Mark Stein. This book tells the true stories that surrounded the reasons our states were given their current borders, and it sheds a lot of light on important aspects of our country's history too. For example, the 49th parallel was chosen to be the northern border of our northern states so that we would have access to the Great Lakes and their fur trade. A lot of the border stories are quite interesting and insightful.

After reading it, use the U.S. map from the appendix and make your own state borders. How would you divide the states? Would they be similar sizes? Would they have panhandles and notches? Include each of the states, but create your own new boundaries for them. Try to consider population, natural resources, and physical boundaries.

☺ ☺ EXPLORATION: Border Dispute

Several years ago Georgia had been in the midst of a drought for several years and so decided to contest their northern border with Tennessee. The border fell about a mile short of reaching the waterfront property of the Tennessee River. The border was supposed to have been drawn up at the 35th parallel according to

BABYLONIANS-MAPPING PEOPLE-HUMANS IN SPACE-POEMS ABOUT PEOPLE

Congress in 1796, but due to poor surveying equipment in 1818, the drawn up border was a little off. If the survey had been accurate then Georgia would indeed have a piece of the river.

Do you think Georgia has any real claim? Should we be adjusting the states' borders all these years later? What would be the implications of changing one state's border? Write an opinion paper about the issue.

☺ ☺ ☺ EXPLORATION: Political Boundaries are Influenced by Geographical Boundaries

Using your student atlas find a physical map of Asia, one that shows no political boundaries but does show rivers, mountains, deserts and so on.

Place a sheet of tracing paper over the map and draw in the boundary lines for countries you make up based on the locations of rivers, mountains, peninsulas and other topographical features. Now compare your imaginary country borders to the real country borders. Are some of them close?

Try this for other continents or for the U.S. States or Canadian Provinces. Are some of the boundaries based on physical geography?

☺ ☺ EXPLORATION: Inset

Sometimes political maps will show an inset. Often the map of the United States is shown with two insets, one for Hawaii and one for Alaska. These two states, which are not connected physically to the other states are put in little boxes, usually in the lower left hand corner. Why do cartographers do this? Find Hawaii and Alaska on a globe. Where are they really? Is the inset drawn at the same scale as the rest of the map?

Additional Layer

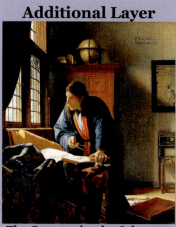

The Geographer by Johannes Vermeer, 1668

Streets by Margret Hofheinz-Döring / Galerie Brigitte Mauch Göppingen, 1989

Portrait of Count of Vaudreuil by Drouais, 1758

Babylonians-Mapping People-Humans in Space-Poems About People

Fabulous Fact
Isolines are lines drawn on a map to show different distributions like this map of Denmark showing average temperatures between May and October.

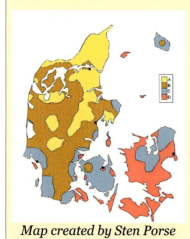

Map created by Sten Porse

Fabulous Fact
A compass rose drawn on a map has 32 points when fully labeled. Naming all 32 points is called "boxing the compass."

Additional Layer
Maps and math go hand in hand when using global grids, compasses, scale, measuring heights and lengths of land features, computing the degrees of latitude and longitude, calculating latitude and direction by the stars, and so on. The great cartographers are also great mathematicians. Practice some map math.

☺ ☺ ☺ EXPEDITION: Map Store
Visit a shop that sells maps near you. Often there are shops dedicated just to maps. Arrange a guided field trip to a store like this. The owner can tell you all about the different types of maps and what they are useful for.

☺ ☺ ☺ EXPLORATION: Create-A-Map
Go online to www.NationalAtlas.gov. This is a site where you can build your own maps using the computer. You can add on exactly the features you want to show. Follow these directions to make a distribution map of your state.
1. Click on the "Map Maker" button in the upper left corner of the National Atlas site.
2. Choose your state from the drop down menu on the upper right.
3. On the menu to the right there are many options to add to your map. Start by adding cities and roads. Click on "Redraw Map."
4. Next choose the "People" tab. Then "Population" and check the box for "Population Density." Click on "Redraw Map."
5. Compare the population density of your state to the neighboring states. See how the the population density of your town compares to the rest of your state.
6. Now play with the map making tools and make all sorts of distribution maps. If you'd like, you can print them out as well.

☺ ☺ EXPLORATION: Water and Population Maps
Make a distribution map showing how much fresh water is available to each country on Earth.

First, make copies of the "Distribution of Fresh Water" map from the end of this unit.

Choose four colors to represent the amount of freshwater available. Explain that "per capita" means how much is available on average to each person who lives in the area. So a country with a decent amount of water but which has a very large population may have less water per capita than a country with about the same amount of available water but a small population. Color the map according to the numbered key.

BABYLONIANS-MAPPING PEOPLE-HUMANS IN SPACE-POEMS ABOUT PEOPLE

What do you learn about the water in the world from this map? Is this what you would have expected? How do you think the amount of water available affects people, populations, politics, war?

☺ ☺ ☺ EXPLORATION: Worldwide Business

Choose a company that does business globally like Coca Cola, McDonald's, Volkswagen, Levi's, Nike, or Microsoft. Research the company and find out where in the world they do business. Create a map showing the per capita distribution of their products.

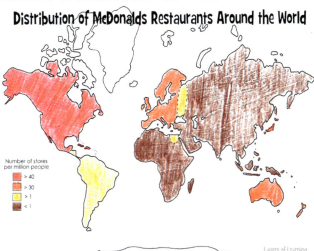

We've included the McDonald's distribution map shown above and also a couple of blank world maps, one with country borders and one without, so you can map any worldwide business you like.

You may also want to include locations of company headquarters or manufacturing plants around the world. How many people are employed by this company and in what countries?

☺ ☺ ☺ EXPLORATION: Trade Treasure Hunt

Go on a "Made In . . ." treasure hunt. Gather objects from around your house and find where they were made. Look up the location in an atlas and plot it on a world map. This activity helps kids become more familiar with countries around the world and helps them to see how we have a global economy. Also you will see a distribution map forming as you add more items. Where do most of the goods in your house come from?

☺ ☺ EXPLORATION: Distribution Map

Explanation

Fixed political borders are a very new condition on Earth. In previous ages the territory under the control of a particular ruler depended on what alliances had been made, which territory had been conquered, who married whom and so on.

There were either rather large empires, made up of the core ruling class and the subdued territories or tiny autonomous city-states or kingdoms. The idea that a particular culture should have its own nation within its own unchangeable boundaries no matter who is in charge changed everything.

Suddenly instead of territory we have nations and we begin to draw heavy dark boundary lines on our maps.

Writer's Workshop

Fictional books that include maps of their own fictional worlds are just cool. Check out *The Chronicles of Narnia, The Lord of the Rings, Treasure Island,* and *The Gammage Cup* for great examples. Make your own map of a fictional world and then write a story that takes place there.

BABYLONIANS-MAPPING PEOPLE-HUMANS IN SPACE-POEMS ABOUT PEOPLE

Famous Folks

Francis Galton invented the first weather map.

He also had other interests, such as the study of eugenics and other exotic belief systems.

Fabulous Facts

Cartography is the art of map making. The word comes from Greek and means: *chartis*=map and *graphein*=write

Another way to refer to "distribution maps" is to call them thematic maps.

Thematic map showing coffee producing countries.

A word on a map that names a place using a non-native word is called an exonym. For example Germany = Deutschland = Allemagne, depending on where you're from.

Find a map of illiteracy rates, birth rates, life expectancies, age distribution or another criteria online. Search for "distribution maps." Study the maps with your student or have them recreate the maps on their own blank line maps. You can do the whole world or choose a continent.

These maps are most often used to make political statements or arguments. Sometimes they tell less than it seems. For example, most of Europe has a lower infant mortality rate than the United States, but this is because European countries often only count live births after two days and the U.S. counts a birth as live at the moment of birth. Since most infant deaths occur within two days of birth, this difference in definitions is very important to the numbers, but the map may not show that. Discuss with your kids how these maps and statistics in general can be used to make certain political statements and discuss your views on the statements they make.

☺ ☺ ☺ **EXPLORATION: World Population**

Make a population map of the world. Keep it simple and use just three shades of the same color. For example you might choose a dark red-orange to represent highly populated areas, a medium orange to represent medium populations and a light yellow-orange to represent lightly populated areas. Use a student atlas to get the information and a world map from the printables at the end of this unit.

☺ ☺ **EXPLORATION: Earth At Night**

Make an "Earth At Night" map. You need a empty cylindrical container like an oatmeal box, paint or construction paper, a printable world map, glue, a nail, and a flashlight.
1. Cover a round oatmeal box with dark construction paper or paint it dark blue, purple or black.
2. Next print out a blank outline map of the earth from the end of this unit. Cut out the continents and glue on to your oatmeal box.
3. Find a map of earth at night from NASA. Search "NASA earth at night" for images. Now poke holes in your world map with the nail at population centers, more holes where the light is brightest.
4. Go into a dark room and turn on a flashlight, placing it up inside your oatmeal box to show the earth at night.

Science: Humans in Space

Part of the character of human beings is that we are never satisfied and always curious. Deep space is one of the last places we have left to physically explore. Though people have been in space, we've never gotten further than the Moon, which is really very close. Most of our exploration in space happens from Earth. Telescopes, and most especially the Hubble Telescope, have phenomenally expanded our knowledge of what's out there. Until just the last few years we suspected there were other planets in other solar systems, but now we've actually seen a few.

But just think of it . . . people have actually stood on the Moon. Wow.

☺ ☺ **EXPLORATION: Parts of a Telescope**
Learn the parts of a telescope and how to focus one. It's easiest to start with something big like the moon if you've never used a telescope before. You can borrow or buy a telescope or purchase a simple "build-your-own" telescope kit for less than $15 from HomeTrainingTools.com. Whether you borrow or buy, take some time to learn about the different features of a telescope. There is a printable worksheet to label the parts of the telescope at the end of this unit.

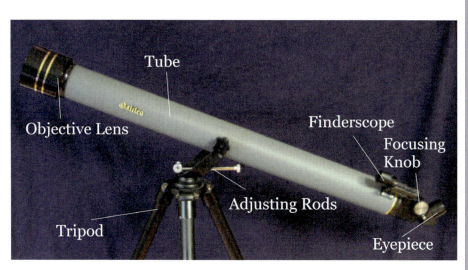

Famous Folks
Ham the Space Chimp was called #65 until after he successfully entered space and landed safely in the Atlantic Ocean. NASA didn't want a named chimp with a personality to make the news if he died en-route. Ham was three years old when he flew to space. He died at the age of twenty-six.

Fabulous Fact
There are two main types of telescopes: reflecting and refracting.

The telescope pictured to the left is a refracting telescope. The telescope below is a reflecting telescopes. They both capture light, but use the light in different ways.

BABYLONIANS-MAPPING PEOPLE-HUMANS IN SPACE-POEMS ABOUT PEOPLE

Explanation

Tired of boring old book reports? Try a Layers of Learning-style book project instead...

1. Imagine YOU are the author of the book you just read. You know it's good. Movie good. Now write a letter to a producer convincing him of why your book would make a great movie. Include the specifics of the storyline that make you think it would be a blockbuster hit, the location you'd like to shoot in, and the actors you think should play your characters.

2. Read a few book reviews in the newspaper and then write your own for your book, worthy of being published in the paper. Hey, maybe you could even send it into the newspaper in your town.

3. Design and sew a costume for the main character in your book. You can make it sized to fit you or a doll you own.

4. Make a collage about your book. Find clippings of pictures and words, anything you can that helps tell the story.

5. Make a quote log with your favorite quotes from the book in it.

Karen

☺ ☺ ☺ EXPEDITION: Space Observatory

There are observatories all over the world. Find out if there is one near you and arrange for a tour. Go to http://www.go-astronomy.com/observatories.htm to search for observatories near you in the United States. If there's not one nearby, do an online tour.

Weston Observatory, Derryfield Park, New Hampshire

☺ ☺ EXPLORATION: Help Wanted

Would you like to work for NASA someday? Find out just what it takes to get a job there. There are lots of careers available, from accountants and computer programmers to scientists and astronauts. One former astronaut, Dr. Sally Ride, gave this advice to kids who may want a future with NASA:

"The most important steps that I followed were studying math and science in school. I was always interested in physics and astronomy and chemistry, and I continued to study those subjects through high school and college and on into graduate school. That's what prepared me for being an astronaut; it actually gave me the qualifications to be selected to be an astronaut. I think the advice that I would give to any kids who want to be astronauts is to make sure that they realize that NASA is looking for people with a whole variety of backgrounds: They are looking for medical doctors, microbiologists, geologists, physicists, electrical engineers. So find something that you really like and then pursue it as far as you can and NASA is apt to be interested in that profession."

Visit the NASAjobs website and peruse their pages. You can search for jobs, read job information, read about how they select their astronauts, and even look at student opportunities. Then use the "What it Takes to Become An Astronaut" page from the printables to record what you find out.

☺ ☺ ☺ EXPLORATION: Space Inventions

When President Eisenhower signed the Space Act, which created NASA, the law stated that NASA's research should benefit all people. Though it's unlikely that you'll ever land on the Moon, the

BABYLONIANS-MAPPING PEOPLE-HUMANS IN SPACE-POEMS ABOUT PEOPLE

technology that has come from NASA has benefited millions of people. Here are just a few of the things we can thank NASA for:
- Invisible braces for your teeth (They are made of the same stuff used to protect the infrared antennae of heat seeking missile trackers.)
- Memory foam mattresses, which were originally created for aircraft seats to lessen landing impact.
- Ear thermometers (based on the technology used to measure the temperature of stars)
- Long distance telecommunication (There are hundreds of satellites orbiting the earth and making this possible, many monitored by NASA to ensure their working order.)
- Certain workout equipment, medical equipment, improved water filtration, improved athletic shoe insoles, improved CAT and MRI scans, and cordless power tools and appliances all have ties to NASA too.

Typically, NASA is not responsible for the actual inventions, but helps contribute to the technology somehow. Often when NASA has a need, they work in conjunction with leaders in a specific field to help fill that need (like when they worked with Black and Decker to improve cordless drills that could then be used in space.)

There are other inventions that are associated with the space program that are actually not spin-offs. Tang, Teflon, and Velcro are often thought to be NASA inventions, but they aren't at all. Tang was on supermarket shelves for several years before it went into space. Teflon was invented in 1938 by DuPont, long before it was used on heat shields and space suits. Velcro was invented in Switzerland in the 1940's.

Can you dream up an invention that could be used in space and also useful for us on earth? Draw a picture or a diagram of your invention. If you want to see some real projects inventors are working on, NASA has a prize program for citizen inventors on their Centennial Challenges website. You can read about what things they are challenging Americans to come up with now.

🙂 🟢 **EXPEDITION: Space Walk in Water**
Go visit your local swimming pool to feel what it's like to walk in space. Get shoulder deep and walk through the water. You can't move quickly; your motion must be slow and deliberate. The resistance is similar to what it feels like in space. In fact, for every hour astronauts spend walking in space, they practice at least 7 hours in a swimming pool called the Neutral Buoyancy Laboratory in NASA's Johnson Space Center in Houston, Texas.

Additional Layer

Stars and other stuff in space send out lots of waves, not just the visible light spectrum we can see. Longer wavelengths in the radio range can be detected with huge radio telescope arrays. Learn about the Very Large Array (VLA).

Very Large Array, New Mexico, USA.

Photo by Hajor and shared under cc license.

Additional Layer

Put together a timeline of space probe missions. Pick one to research more thoroughly.

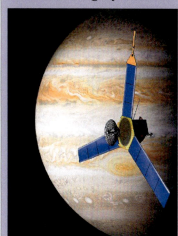

Juno Space Probe, image by NASA

Babylonians-Mapping People-Humans in Space-Poems About People

Famous Folks

Barbara Askins was a chemist hired by NASA to experiment with new ways of developing film for photographs taken in space and of space objects. She created a process to successfully restore images that were underexposed and would otherwise have been useless. Her discoveries led to better uses for X-ray technology and the restoration of old pictures.

Additional Layer

How far is it from the Earth to the Moon? It takes a laser light about 2.5 seconds to be sent to the Moon and relect back to Earth. If light travels at 299,792,458 meters per second (approximately 186,282 miles per second) how far away is the Moon? Remember the light is traveling both directions so you'll need to divide the answer in half.

Astronauts go on space walks to let them repair equipment, test new equipment, and conduct experiments outside of their spacecraft. They wear spacesuits, which function as miniature spacecrafts. Now imagine you are walking through that same water while wearing an enormous spacesuit and trying to repair intricate machinery. Your spacewalk mission just got a bit harder!

NASA Neutral Buoyancy Lab at the Johnson Space Center in Houston

☺ ☻ **EXPERIMENT: Is There Zero Gravity In Space?**
It seems obvious. Astronauts float around in their space ships up there, so there must not be any gravity, right?
Not so fast. Gravity is the force between any two objects that have mass. There is mass in space (you, the planets, the stars), so there must be gravity also. The Moon feels the effect of the Earth's gravity. The Earth feels the effect of the Sun's gravity. There is gravity in space. The effects of gravity do lessen with distance, but astronauts are only a few hundred miles above the surface of the Earth. A person who weighs 160 pounds on Earth would still weigh about 140 pounds at that distance. Still plenty to hit the floor, so why do they float?

They float because they are in free fall. The shuttle is falling toward the Earth in a circle. As long as it doesn't slow down it will never hit the earth though. That's what an orbit is, it's falling in a circle.

BABYLONIANS-MAPPING PEOPLE-HUMANS IN SPACE-POEMS ABOUT PEOPLE

Try this experiment outside or over a tub:
1. Get a paper cup and poke a hole in the bottom with a pencil.
2. Fill the cup with water. Water should drip out of the hole, because gravity is pulling it toward earth.
3. Now drop the cup from a high place. Watch the dripping water carefully.
4. What happens while the cup is falling?

When things are free falling they are weightless. Perhaps you've experienced a bit of this in an elevator, or on a roller coaster or a free fall ride at the amusement park.

Astronauts in training aboard the "Vomit Comet", a plane that performs a parabolic dive to give astronauts experience with weightlessness while still in the atmosphere of Earth.

☺ ☺ ☺ **EXPERIMENT: A One Man Spaceship**

An astronaut's spacesuit is a spaceship designed with all the stuff that humans need to stay alive in the hostile environment of space. Brainstorm things the spacesuit would have to take into account: temperature regulation, pressure regulation, air to breathe, a place to go potty . . . you can probably think of more.

Design an experiment to see what types of materials make better insulation. Use a heat lamp and thermometers plus various insulating materials like cloth, fiberglass insulation, foil, rubber, synthetic batting and so on. Try layering more than one type of insulation. Then look up information on what the astronauts suits are

Additional Layer

When you gotta go, you gotta go. How do astronauts go to the bathroom in space if everything floats? Find out about the vacuum technology that makes it possible. Showering presents a similar problem since the water doesn't flow down. Go research how astronauts on the space station do it!

Famous Folks

Eileen Collins is a retired Air Force Test pilot and NASA astronaut. She has been decorated many times, flew four space flights and commanded the mission STS-93 in 1999.

Photo by NASA.

Fabulous Fact

This is a 1967 U.S. stamp depicting an astronaut space walk.

Babylonians-Mapping People-Humans in Space-Poems About People

Writer's Workshop

Have your kids choose a space pioneer to make a trading card of. You will need an image of the pioneer and some card stock or other thick paper. Glue the image to one side of the card, then on the back side write down several facts about the person. Include things like when they were born, which country they were from (or worked for), what their major accomplishments were, and when they died.

Though the card itself doesn't hold much information, in order to find even that little bit the student will have to do quite a bit of reading and learning about their space pioneer. Share the pioneers with one another.

On the Web

Visit http://www.ss42.com/pt-space.html for links to tons of free printable paper models of space equipment online.

Make sure to grab the Space Activity Book at:
http://www.nasa.gov/audience/forkids/activities/Activities_Collection_archive_1.html

really made of.

😊 🟢 EXPLORATION: An Astronaut's Suitcase

Most of the things an astronaut takes along to go into space are dictated by NASA. On the shuttle there are special lockers that hold an astronaut's clothes, food, and personal items. There isn't a lot of room for extras, but if you were an astronaut and could take just one special item into space with you, what would you take? Why? Write about it in your writer's notebook.

😊 🟢 EXPERIMENT: Refracting Lenses

Most of the space exploration humans do is not in person, but is done through the aid of telescopes. Refracting telescopes use large lenses that collect the light from stars and reflect it. The image comes though upside down.

Try this: Take two magnifying lenses. Hold one out at arm's length and focus on an object fifteen or twenty feet away. You will see the object upside down in the lens.

Now hold a second lens up to the first. The magnifying power is much greater with two lenses.

😊 🟢 🔵 EXPERIMENT: Lunar Laser Ranging

When the Apollo 11 astronauts landed on the Moon they did experiments there and left some equipment behind so ongoing experiments could be done from Earth. One of those was the Lunar Laser Ranging Experiment, which is a fancy way of saying "measuring the distance between the Earth and Moon."

Babylonians-Mapping People-Humans in Space-Poems About People

The astronauts left retro-reflectors on the Moon and scientists since then have been sending lasers at the reflectors. The time it takes for the laser light to come back helps scientists to measure the distance since we know how fast light travels. You can make your own retro-reflector.

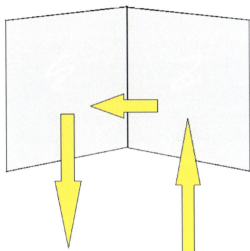

You need two mirrors and a flashlight in a darkened room. Tape the mirrors together so they open like a book. Set the mirrors up facing you and point a flashlight at one of the mirrors. Now adjust the mirrors until a spot of light shines back and hits the front of your shirt. You've created a retro-reflector, just like the astronauts.

☺ ☺ ● **EXPLORATION: Space Probe Missions**

A space probe is an unmanned scientific mission sent into space for the purpose of gathering information or performing a specific experiment. Make a list of the major space probe missions in chronological order along with the country that sponsored them and the information that was obtained.

Voyager Probe, launched by NASA 1977

☺ ● **EXPLORATION: I Learned About People in Space**

Use the notebooking pages from the printables section for the writing assignments or to write about the things you learned during this unit.

Explanation

Homeschool vs. Public School

Is one method superior to another? Absolutely and unequivocally. But the one which is superior depends on the circumstances of the student, the family, and the local school.

Homeschool may be perfect for the Andersons and public school may be the right choice for the Browns.

Instead of condemning and worrying and obsessing about the choices of the family next door we should rejoice that we have choices, that we all care so much about educating kids, and that we all have so much in common. In any case and all cases (except extreme neglect or abuse) freedom of parental choice should be our standard and we should be cheering each other on and supporting each other and feeling positively toward one another. Hooray for the parents and teachers in every environment who are doing their best for the kids under their care. Props to you all!!!

Michelle

BABYLONIANS-MAPPING PEOPLE-HUMANS IN SPACE-POEMS ABOUT PEOPLE

THE ARTS: POEMS ABOUT PEOPLE

Additional Layer

Younger kids may not understand rhyme. Take some time learning about and practicing rhyming. Read some rhyming poetry and identify the rhyming words.

Teaching Tip

Work on memorizing almost constantly, whether it's the times tables or a poem, memorization exercises mental muscles and makes one more agile. During this unit choose a poem or two. For motivation have a reward for a poem committed to memory.

Additional Layer

Kids shouldn't just read "kids poetry." Introduce them to some grown-up poets like:

Walt Whitman

Robert Frost

Edgar Allen Poe

Maya Angelou

Emily Dickinson

William Shakespeare

Edgar Guest

William Wordsworth

Poetry is just a way of having fun with language. One of the troubles with teaching poetry is that it really can't be taught. You can see a lot of examples and read a lot of great poems, but in the end, a poem has to come from within the poet. Throw out the rules you think you know about poetry. Every single poem does not have to rhyme. It doesn't have to have rhythm. It doesn't have to be long or serious. Poems can take many forms and even shapes. They can be funny. They can make you think. Throughout many of the poetry units you'll see formulas for writing poems, but these should be a beginning place, a jumping off point for whatever poetry YOU want to write. They help us get a start instead of feeling stuck. After the ideas are flowing, kids should feel free to move on however they want to. Experiment. Play with words. Write what you feel and think and dream. Because that is what makes a poet.

Poems about people can be funny because, well, people are funny! Biography poems, Clerihews, and name poems are all great places to start as you explore the world of poetry.

 **EXPLORATION: The Poetry of Shel Silverstein**

Reading poetry should come before writing poetry, kind of like warming up before the big game. Shel Silverstein writes terrific poems that kids love. Flip open one of his poetry books and read to your heart's content. He frequently writes silly poems about imaginary people that would be a great jumping off place for writing poems about people.

BABYLONIANS-MAPPING PEOPLE-HUMANS IN SPACE-POEMS ABOUT PEOPLE

EXPLANATION: In Love With Poetry
Before ever asking kids to write poetry they should read lots of it. My kids are given a poem every week that we add to little memorization booklets. We read through them and practice, and by the end of the week they can recite the poem by heart. When we read longer poems that I don't expect them to memorize we do an activity to go along with the poem instead. Here's one we did with "My Shadow" by Robert Louis Stevenson. The poem is about shadows, so I traced my daughter's silhouette on dark paper. She cut it out and attached the poem.

The bottom line? Read, read, read, read, and read some more. Then when you have them start writing it, make it just as fun as the funny poems you started reading in the first place.

Robert Frost said, "A poem begins in delight and ends in wisdom." I think of this sentiment often when planning poetry lessons. Delight and wisdom . . . both should have an equally important place in poetry.

Karen

😊 😊 😊 **EXPLORATION: Name Poem**
A name poem is a poem about you! Well, really it's a poem about your name, but it should reflect you too, so get ready to describe yourself poetically! All you need to do is fill in each blank:

Line 1: _____
     (Your first name)
Line 2: It means _____
     (3 adjectives that describe you)
Line 3: It is the number _____
     (your favorite number)
Line 4: It is like _____
     (describe your favorite color without actually saying the color!)
Line 5: It is _____
     (a memory that makes you smile)
Line 6: It is the memory of _____
     (someone who is important to you)

Explanation

To teach about rhyme, first show them how it's done. Give them a simple word ending.

-AT

Then demonstrate how to go through the alphabet creating some words (and maybe even a few nonsense words) using the ending.

AT BAT CAT DAT FAT GAT HAT MAT (G)NAT PAT RAT SAT TAT VAT ZAT

Once they've practiced with a few of their own endings, let them finish some sentences with rhymes:

The picnic was taken right over by ants. Boy, I am grateful they left me _____.
(rhyme with ants)

Give me some money. I know what I'll do. Take me to the mall and I'll buy _____.
(rhyme with "do)

Outer space is really cool. The aliens here all love _____.
(rhyme with cool)

BABYLONIANS-MAPPING PEOPLE-HUMANS IN SPACE-POEMS ABOUT PEOPLE

Famous Folks

E. Clerihew Bentley invented the Clerihew form of poetry while a boy at school. He wrote a volume of poetry called *Biography For Beginners*. Besides the funny poems he wrote a famous detective novel called *Trent's Last Case*.

Clerihews by Clerihew

The art of Biography
Is different from Geography.
Geography is about maps,
But Biography is about chaps.

Sir Christopher Wren
Said, 'I am going to dine with some men.
If anyone calls
Say I am designing St. Paul's.'

John Stuart Mill,
By a mighty effort of will,
Overcame his natural bonhomie
And wrote 'Principles of Political Economy.'

What I like about Clive
Is that he is no longer alive.
There is a great deal to be said
For being dead.

Edward the Confessor
Slept under the dresser.
When that began to pall,
He slept in the hall.

Chapman & Hall
Swore not at all.
Mr. Chapman's yea was yea,
And Mr Hall's nay was nay.

It was a weakness of Voltaire's
To forget to say his prayers,
And one which to his shame
He never overcame.

Line 7: Who taught me _____
             (2 abstract concepts like integrity or love)

Line 8: When s/he _____
(something the person from line 6 did that displayed the qualities from line 7)

Line 9: My name is _____
                 (your first name again)

Line 10: It means: _____
             (tell something important that you believe in a sentence)

Here's one I once wrote. It's more on the serious side, but reflects what I was experiencing at that time of my life.

> *Karen*
> *It means patient, happy, peaceful*
> *It is the number 5*
> *It is like snow on Christmas morning.*
> *It is camping at the ocean.*
> *It is the memory of my baby daughter*
> *who taught me perseverance and strength*
> *When she died before I was ready to say goodbye.*
> *My name is Karen;*
> *It means living every day full of love.*

Now you give it a try in your writer's notebook. If I wrote 10 name poems about myself they would all be different depending on what I'm thinking about, what I'm experiencing, and how I feel. People have lots of sides and lots of layers.

You can also write poems about other people's names, so don't limit yourself! It could be about anyone you know and want to write about.

😊 😊 😊 EXPLORATION: Clerihew

There are a few rules for Clerihews (Remember, in poetry you're allowed to throw rules right out the door if you don't like them!)

Rule #1 – They are four lines long.

Rule #2 – You usually have the first 2 lines rhyme with each other, and the last two lines rhyme with each other.

Rule #3 – The first line ends with the name of the person you're writing about and the second line ends with a word that rhymes with their name.

Rule #4 – Keep it light and funny.

BABYLONIANS-MAPPING PEOPLE-HUMANS IN SPACE-POEMS ABOUT PEOPLE

*I have the nicest dad
but darn it, he is mad.
What made him go boo hoo?
The dog pooped in his shoe.*

Here's one more for you:

*Doctor Rick
Makes me sick.
His needle poke
Makes me croak.*

EXPLANATION: Rhyming Help
Sometimes coming up with the perfect rhyme can be a struggle! You can use online rhyming dictionaries as a great resource. Just type in the word you want to rhyme with and all the possibilities will appear. Sometimes the rhymes still just don't work out and the poem needs to take another direction, but often just taking a minute to look up the word in an online rhyming dictionary will get kids out of a rut and going again.

☺ ☺ ☺ **EXPLORATION: Biography Poem**
A biography poem is really similar to a name poem. They tend to be a little more generic, focusing on biographical information more than life experiences. Here's a basic formula to jump off from:

    Line 1- First name
    Line 2- 4 adjectives to describe you
    Line 3- Brother/Sister or Son/Daughter of...
    Line 4- Lover of...(1-3 nouns)
    Line 5- Who feels...(1-3 things)
    Line 6- Who needs...(1-3 things)
    Line 7- Who gives...(1-3 things)
    Line 8- Who fears...(1-3 things)
    Line 9- Who would like to...(1-3 things)
    Line 10- Resident of (your city and state)
    Line 11- Last name

Here's an example:

Hannah
Blonde, brunette, famous, unknown
Daughter of Billy Ray
Lover of singing, concerts, and lyrics that almost give her away
Who feels silly
Who needs friends
Who gives grief to her brother

Additional Layer

Biography poems can be used as a book project or alternative book report. Just choose a character from the book to write the poem about.

Memorization Station

*Invicticus
by W.E. Henley*

Out of the night that covers me,
Black as the Pit from pole to pole,
I thank whatever gods may be
For my unconquerable soul.

In the fell clutch of circumstance
I have not winced nor cried aloud.
Under the bludgeonings of chance
My head is bloody, but unbowed.

Beyond this place of wrath and tears
Looms but the Horror of the shade,
And yet the menace of the years
Finds, and shall find, me unafraid.

It matters not how strait the gate,
How charged with punishments the scroll,
I am the master of my fate:
I am the captain of my soul.

Babylonians-Mapping People-Humans in Space-Poems About People

Teaching Tip
Being culturally literate means understanding references that are common to our culture. When you hear a quote from Shakespeare you should know it's Shakespeare, and so on. Expose your kids to stories, poems, literature, art, and music that form the basis for English speaking culture.

Additional Layer
Just as art is very subjective, so is poetry. We all have our favorites. Here are a few of my favorite children's poets:

- Shel Silverstein
- Jack Prelutsky
- Bruce Lansky
- A.A. Milne
- Judith Viorst

Head to the library and check out several collections of poems. You'll find everything from classic to brand new and from sad to very humorous. Find some of your own favorites.

Who fears being discovered
Who would like to be known as Miley
Resident of TV sets all over America
Montana

You may notice that I broke some of the rules (well, bent them anyway) when I wrote the example. That's okay. You can too. You can write one about yourself, someone you know, or someone famous. Give it a try.

😊 😊 😊 EXPLORATION: Audience-Participation Poem
Try an audience participation poem by reading a poem that you've assigned call-outs for. Look for one about people during this unit.

You can check out any poetry book that has longer children's poems in it for this activity. Ahead of time, scan through the poem for words that are repeated, and then assign each of those words an action or a call-out.

For example, a poem about the wild west might have words like:
    cowboy (say yee-haw!)
    horse (yell giddy-up)
    hat (tip your hat)

Each time you come across one of those words, the audience will call out or do their action.

😊 😊 😊 EXPLORATION: Self-Portrait Poems
You are going to describe the way you look in this poem, creating a word-version portrait, or picture, of yourself. First of all, touch your hair. What does it feel like? (Soft thread? Dry grass? Porcupine quills? Fluffy feathers?) You also may be describing the length or color. Your hair may be like a waterfall falling from your head in long waves, or like a pine cone with tiny humps and bumps all over. Your hair may be like glowing sun or just like the chocolate bar that melts all over a s'more. Once you've had some practice describing features, you're ready to start writing your self-portrait poem.

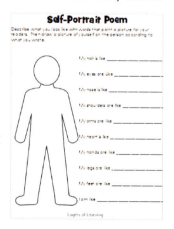

Use the printable template from the end of this unit to pen your poem.

BABYLONIANS-MAPPING PEOPLE-HUMANS IN SPACE-POEMS ABOUT PEOPLE

☺ ☺ ☺ **EXPLORATION: When I Was Young. . .**

Even young kids used to be younger than they are now, so anyone can write a poem like this. Begin by thinking of a memory from your past. I immediately thought of piano lessons from my childhood, because now I'm a piano teacher and that role helps define who I am. Choose a memory that is somehow telling about who you are and write a free verse poem about it.

Free verse just means a poem that doesn't need to rhyme or have any particular form. You're basically just relating a memory in a concise way. Here's the one I wrote about my childhood piano lessons:

<u>Piano Lessons On Tuesdays</u>
When I was young I went to piano lessons on Tuesdays.
The old woman was
GENTLE.
When I didn't have time to practice she
UNDERSTOOD.
When I made a mistake she taught me that mistakes make me
GROW.
She didn't mind that I bit my fingernails and said my hands were
BEAUTIFUL.
Her rose stained glass windows made my eyes
WONDER.
Her huge, black grand piano made me
SING.
The dim room with a glowing lamp over the keys made me
CALM.
When I left on Tuesdays, my heart was
AGLOW.

Now I teach piano on Tuesdays and all the other days too.

On The Web
Go to the superteacher website for a fun people poetry activity about how we get our features from family genetics. Visit the site and click on family features.

http://www.superteacherworksheets.com/poems.html

Additional Layer

Create a thumbprint autobiography about yourself. Use an inkpad to stamp your thumbprint, enlarge it with a photocopier to make it more visible, then write all about yourself along the lines of your thumbprint.

Coming up next . . .

Unit 1-6
The Levant
Physical Earth
Laws of Motion
List Poems

36

BABYLONIANS-MAPPING PEOPLE-HUMANS IN SPACE-POEMS ABOUT PEOPLE

My Ideas For This Unit:

Title: _____   Topic: _____

_____

_____

_____

_____

_____

_____

_____

_____

Title: _____   Topic: _____

_____

_____

_____

_____

_____

_____

_____

_____

_____

_____

Title: _____   Topic: _____

_____

_____

_____

_____

_____

_____

_____

_____

_____

BABYLONIANS-MAPPING PEOPLE-HUMANS IN SPACE-POEMS ABOUT PEOPLE

My Ideas For This Unit:

Title: _____   Topic: _____

_____
_____
_____
_____
_____
_____
_____
_____
_____

Title: _____   Topic: _____

_____
_____
_____
_____
_____
_____
_____
_____
_____
_____

Title: _____   Topic: _____

_____
_____
_____
_____
_____
_____
_____
_____
_____

Ishtar Gate

Ishtar Gate was built by King Nebuchadnezzar, the Babylonian king. It was the main entrance to the city of Babylon. It was named after the goddess Ishtar. King Nebuchadnezzar also restored the Temple of Marduk and the Hanging Gardens. He wanted to make Babylon beautiful. At first the Ishtar Gate was one of the Seven Wonders of the World, but it was replaced by the Lighthouse of Alexandria. Some ancients believed that it was so exquisite that it, along with the walls of Babylon, should still be considered a wonder. Color its walls blue and the animals brown and yellow, just like the original Ishtar Gate.

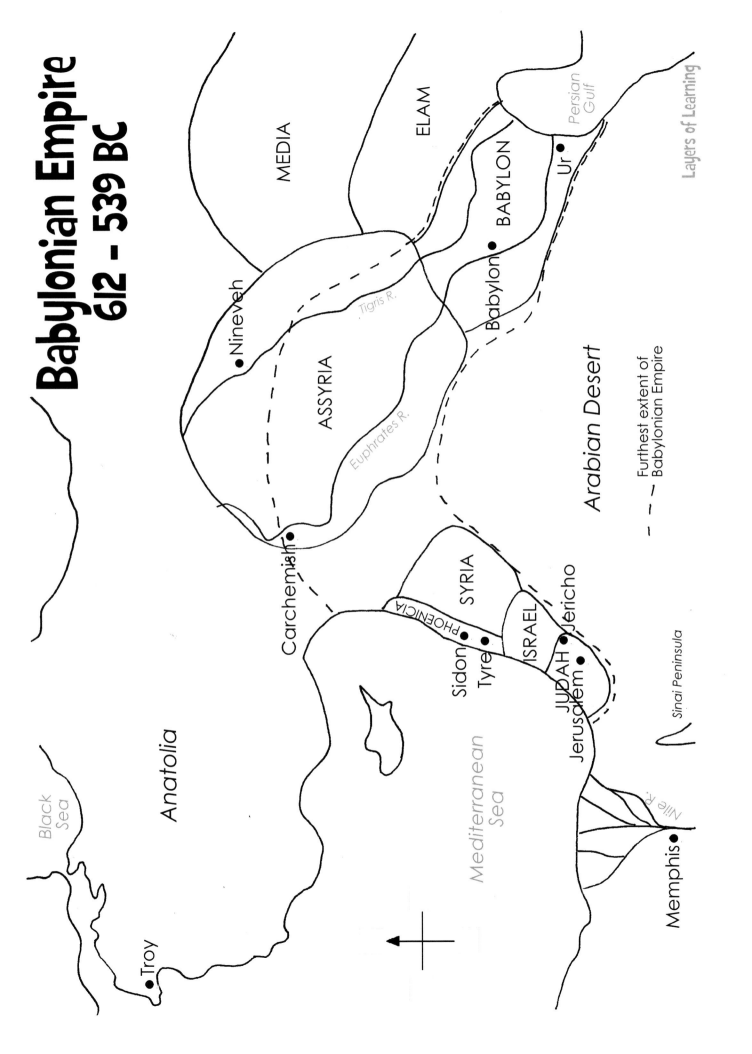

Babylonian Calendar

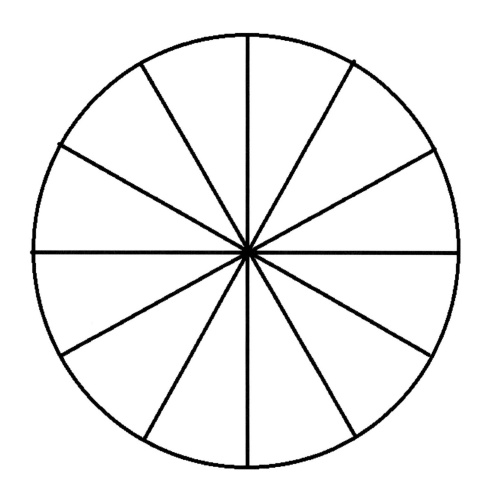

Makausa Addari   Simanu   Tisritum   Sabatu
Addaru   Dumuzu   Samna   summer/fall
Nisanu   Abu   Kislimu   spring/summer
Aru   Ululu   Tebetum   winter

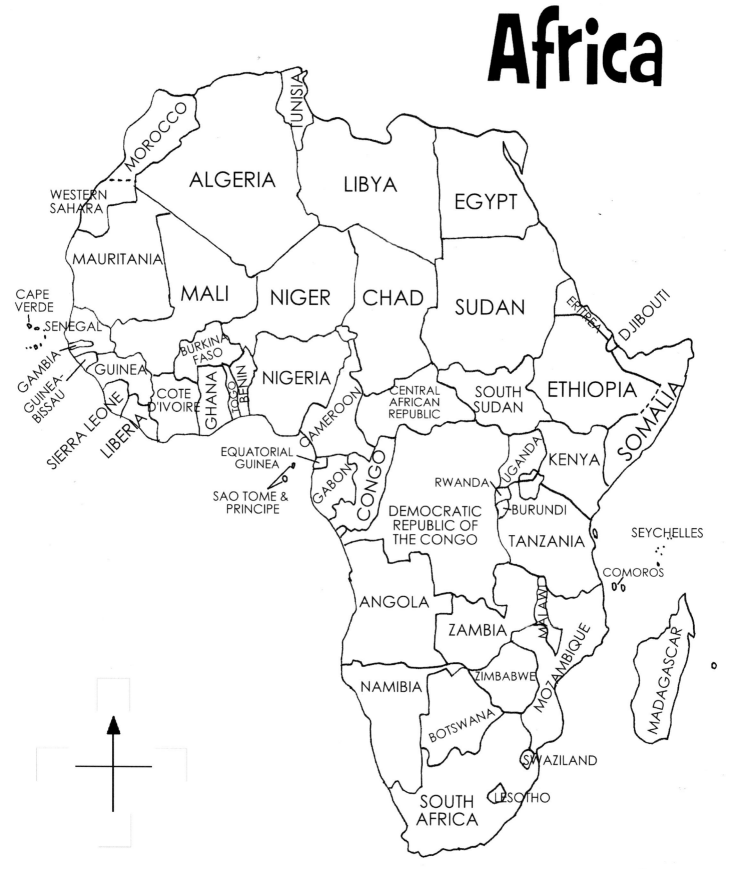

Distribution of Fresh Water

Layers of Learning

Amount of fresh
water per capita

1	> 50,000 m³
2	> 5000 m³
3	> 1000 m³
4	< 1000 m³

Distribution of McDonalds Restaurants Around the World

Layers of Learning

Number of stores
per million people

1	> 40
2	> 30
3	> 1
4	< 1

The World

Layers of Learning

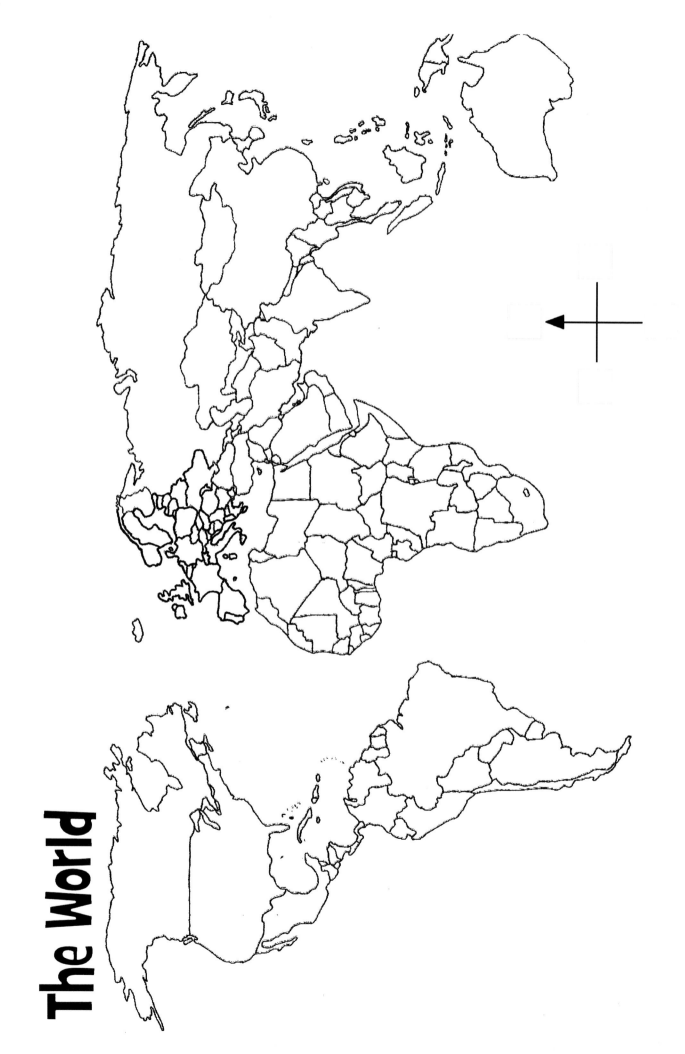

Word Bank

finderscope   tripod   adjusting rods

objective lens   tube   focusing knob

eyepiece

Parts of a Telescope

Layers of Learning

What It Takes To Become An Astronaut . . .

Draw yourself as an astronaut and create a flag that represents the skills you think you have that would help you be a great space traveler. Becoming an astronaut isn't easy. Find out what it takes to become an astronaut . . .

What kind of an education should I get?

What specific fields is NASA looking for?

Do I need any special skills?

What percentage of people living on our planet have actually traveled into space?

What other jobs does NASA have that would interest me?

Read the stories of at least 3 NASA astronauts and find out how they became astronauts.

Layers of Learning

Layers of Learning

Self-Portrait Poem

Describe what you look like with words that paint a picture for your readers. Then draw a picture of yourself on the person according to what you wrote.

My hair is like _____

My eyes are like _____

My nose is like _____

My shoulders are like _____

My arms are like _____

My heart is like _____

My hands are like _____

My legs are like _____

My feet are like _____

I am like _____

Layers of Learning

ABOUT THE AUTHORS

Karen & Michelle . . .
Mothers, sisters, teachers, women who are passionate about educating kids.
We are dedicated to lifelong learning.

Karen, a mother of four, who has homeschooled her kids for more than eight years with her husband, Bob, has a bachelor's degree in child development with an emphasis in education. She lives in Utah where she gardens, teaches piano, and plays an excruciating number of board games with her kids. Karen is our resident Arts expert and English guru {most necessary as Michelle regularly and carelessly mangles the English language and occasionally steps over the bounds of polite society}.

Michelle and her husband, Cameron, homeschooling now for over a decade, teach their six boys on their ten acres in beautiful Idaho country. Michelle earned a bachelor's in biology, making her the resident Science expert, though she is mocked by her friends for being the Botanist with the Black Thumb of Death. She also is the go-to for History and Government. She believes in staying up late, hot chocolate, and a no whining policy. We both pitch in on Geography, in case you were wondering, and are on a continual quest for knowledge.

Visit our constantly updated blog for tons of free ideas, free printables, and more cool stuff for sale:
www.Layers-of-Learning.com

Made in the USA
San Bernardino, CA
31 October 2018